Storms & Blizzards

Written and illustrated by
Mary Micallef

Cover by Phil Brevick

Copyright © Good Apple, Inc., 1985

GOOD APPLE, INC.
BOX 299
CARTHAGE, IL 62321-0299

Copyright © Good Apple, Inc., 1985

ISBN No. 0-86653-321-4

Printing No. 98765432

**GOOD APPLE, INC.
BOX 299
CARTHAGE, IL 62321-0299**

The purchase of this book entitles the buyer to reproduce student activity pages for classroom use only. Any other use requires written permission from Good Apple, Inc.

All rights reserved. Printed in the United States of America.

TABLE OF CONTENTS

A Word to the Teacher iv
Pre-Unit Activities v
Extension vi

Introduction
Patterns in Nature 1
Weather Folklore 2
A Weather Legacy of My Own 3
Weather That Made History 4
Stories About Weather and People 5
People Can Change the Weather 6

Factors That Affect the Weather
Spinning Around the Sun 7
Atmosphere 8
Worldwide and Local Winds 9

Thunderstorms
Rumbles Come Tumbling 10
Thunderstorms 11
Supercooled Puzzle 12
Lightning 13
Lightning Safety Precautions 14
Inside a Thunderstorm 15

Snow
Some Cold Hard Facts 16
Bergy Bits and Growlers 17
Snow's Value in the Natural Cycle 18
Scientific Root Words 19
William Bentley and the Snowflake 20
Snowflakes 21

Teacher Pages
Added Dimensions 22
Designs in a Winter Motif 23

Winter Weather
Winter Survival: Migration and Hibernation 24
Adapting to Winter Climates 25
Winter Storms: Cause and Effects 26
Ready or Not, Here I Come! 27
Monitoring Worldwide Weather 28
Snow and More Snow 29
Cold American Winters 30
The Story of Snow at Donner Pass 31
Icy Winter Driving 32
Winter Storm Car Kit 33
Winter Killers 34
Windchill Factor 35
Weather Watch and Warnings 36
Winter Storm Safety Rules 37
Winter Weather Word Search 38
Measuring Heat and Cold 39

Answer Key 40
Index 41
Bibliography 42

With special thanks for good friends and hot soup on stormy winter nights, to Margret and Peter at Zum Alten Deutschen, Bitburg, Germany.

iii

A WORD TO THE TEACHER

OVERVIEW

Storms & Blizzards is a unit of lessons and activities that provides students with a basic understanding of the causes and consequences of these seasonal natural disasters. Children learn about weather patterns and systems, basic factors that influence weather in an area, weather folklore and history, thunderstorms, and major winter weather fronts.

Every day people make decisions based on the weather. Children enjoy discovering more about their own choices as their weather awareness grows. People significantly alter the weather in an area by the changes they make in the topography of the land. Scientists are learning more about purposely changing weather patterns. Individuals have always adjusted weather in their immediate environment by the way they build and heat their homes and the clothes they choose to wear.

When violent weather approaches, immediate steps can be taken to protect life and property. *Storms & Blizzards* includes a study of weather warning systems, storm, lightning, and blizzard safety rules, and weather terminology. Students learn how weather is monitored around the world and how weather forecasting is affected by hundreds of constantly changing factors.

FORMAT

Information and activities in this book are designed for classroom teachers to be used in correlation with a science unit or as a supplement to a science curriculum. It can be adapted to meet each teacher's specific classroom needs and unique teaching style. The units are arranged sequentially, but activities can be extended or omitted according to student interests and abilities.

With an emphasis on scientific reading skills, most lessons are followed by three multiple choice questions. The questions encourage comprehension, evaluation, and application skills by requiring students to look for cause and effect, to make predictions based on information in the selection, and to draw conclusions supported by the evidence presented. Classroom discussion of these questions enables students to review and extend what they have learned in the lesson. An answer key is on page 40.

PRE-UNIT ACTIVITIES

Pre-unit, or early-unit, activities provide motivation as well as background experience for students. Brainstorming and open-ended discussions can be valuable to both teacher and student. Group interaction often lets the teacher know both the accurate information and the misconceptions that students have about the topic. Lessons can then be altered or extended throughout the unit to meet individual class needs.

Some pre-unit weather activities might include some of the following:
1. Brainstorm a list of weather words on the chalkboard with the class. As ideas begin to slow down, challenge the students to try starting with **arid** (hot and dry) and going all the way to **zephyr** (a mild breeze).
2. Classify the list of weather words according to season, state of matter, or even parts of speech. Are there adjectives like humid, blustery, or frigid? How many other words for weather does the list include (hail, ice, snow, fog)?
3. Have students make a bulletin board of illustrated weather words. **Icy** can be drawn as dripping icicles, for example, or **hot** with a blazing sun for the **o**.
4. Suggest that each student keep a personal list of weather words in his notebook or weather journal. Listen for additional words in songs, on the radio, or in conversation. Watch for weather words in other classes, magazines, and books.
5. Create weather awareness by talking and writing about the way weather affects the clothes people wear (sandals and shorts versus boots and sweaters), the foods people eat (lemonade versus hot chocolate), the ways people spend their leisure time (tennis and swimming versus football and ice skating).
6. An innovative and challenging spelling packet might include at least twenty of the words that students will encounter through either **Storms** or **Winter Weather** studies. Try word searches, scrambled words, and mix and match definitions. Students will understand the unit better if the terminology is clear from the beginning.
7. Let children share their own weather experiences with each other. What's the hottest day they can remember? Has anyone ever been afraid of the weather? Can cloudy days affect the way we feel? Has anyone ever been disappointed in the weather? What's a favorite thing to do on rainy days?

EXTENSION

A. **Read to Find Out** sections encourage students to independently pursue topics pertaining to their own interests, talents, and capabilities. If children are encouraged to share what they have discovered on a daily basis, their classmates will also benefit from the enrichment. A bulletin board of student posters, book recommendations, incredible facts, drawings and maps is an excellent vehicle for enabling children to learn from each other.

Most books about mythology are found in libraries under Dewey Decimal 291. Many books about storms and blizzards are in the 551 section. Since information is so rapidly updated in scientific areas, the books since 1975 are probably most useful. Current information is always available in the *Readers' Guide to Periodical Literature*, an indispensable resource for science and social studies exploration.

Safety information can be requested from the Superintendent of Documents, U.S. Government Printing Office, Washington, D.C. 20402. Students may also write directly to the National Oceanic and Atmospheric Administration, Department of Commerce, Washington, D.C. 20230. Many pamphlets and safety posters can be ordered in classroom sets.

A starting bibliography of excellent supplementary reading material is found at the back of this book as well as throughout the units. The classroom library can provide a wealth of answers to extraordinary questions as students become involved with *Storms & Blizzards*. Creatively illustrated, dynamic additions in folklore and fiction are assets. *A January Fog Will Freeze a Hog* by Hubert Davis (Crown Publishers, 1977) is excellent! Don't forget storm poetry, music and art.

B. As with any relevant topic, children who keep a notebook or journal of information, quotes, resources, notes, questions, and discoveries will have a permanent summary of the subject that personalizes and perserves their study. Several pages in *Storms & Blizzards* are dedicated to a beginning understanding of scientific terms, root words, and classifications. While students would hardly be expected to memorize these words and definitions, a familiarity with them is surely an asset in our information society. Children need terminology as tools for increasing their personal knowledge and awareness.

C. Some parts of *Storms & Blizzards* are designed to stimulate children's interest and involvement. "Bergy Bits and Growlers" or "Some Cold Hard Facts" might be presented as whole class discussions with children gathered in a listening circle (away from the listening barriers of desk and distance!) on the floor near the teacher. Brainstorming is welcomed! Children have an opportunity for getting excited about what's coming up.

Creative science activities found in most science series teachers' manuals and in books like Good Apple's *Creative, Hands-on Science Experiences* by Jerry DeBruin certainly add to student understanding through participation and exploration.

Name _____

PATTERNS IN NATURE

People have always looked for ways to know more about the world around them. The more they understood about natural events, the better were their chances of survival. Early communities needed to know when to move on to warmer lands or how much wood to gather for the winter. If they knew when to plant crops, their chances for a successful harvest improved.

The wisest people, especially those who had lived a long and productive life, began to recognize patterns in nature. It was easy to learn that February is usually cold and that March is usually windy. People didn't all use the same calendar, but they saw the phases of the moon and the changes of the season in pretty much the same way all across the Northern Hemisphere.

The American Indians called January the Lone Wolf Moon. It was often bitterly cold. While many animals hibernated or moved south, the wolf would continue to roam and hunt through the long nights and across the frozen plains. February became known as the Snow Moon. Can you imagine why it got its name?

March was named for Mars, the Roman god of war. With its roaring winds, sudden storms, and unpredictable weather, it seemed that the forces of nature were fighting with each other during that month.

If you were naming the months from your experience in your part of the world, what names would you give to describe the patterns you recognize in the seasons? Try a few months, and compare them with your classmates. Try to draw a symbol for each month that shows what you have learned to expect during that particular part of the year.

January _____ May_____ September _____

February_____ June _____ October _____

March_____ July_____ November _____

April _____ August _____ December _____

Name _____

WEATHER FOLKLORE

Through the years, people discovered more and more about the weather. Early hunters, sailors, fishermen, and farmers needed specific information to plan their day. They learned to read the clouds.

In the third century B.C., Theophrastus wrote the *Book of Signs* with over 200 ways to tell about rain, wind, and good weather. A red sunrise, rings around the sun or moon, and special kinds of clouds foretold rain, according to the Greek philosopher-scientist. Many of Theophrastus' weather signs were used as the basis of study for hundreds of years in different climates around the world.

Sometimes people would make up a rhyme to help them remember the weather signs that they observed. "In the morning mountains, in the evening fountains" is an old English saying that tells about the relationship between big, mountainous clouds and rain.

In addition to signs in the sky, people saw patterns between the behavior of animals and the kind of weather that followed. American and European folklore contains hundreds of short verses or weather rhymes that describe these relationships.

"When sheep gather in a huddle, tomorrow we'll have a puddle" is another bit of weather lore that began in England. It is true that sheep usually bunch together before a storm or cold weather. Shepherds have a lot of time to observe the behavior of their animals, and they take a special interest in protecting their flocks from the elements.

"Rainbow in the morning, shepherds take warning. Rainbow at night, shepherd's delight." What do you think this old rhyme is saying? Why?

Benjamin Franklin included dozens of weather predictors in his almanacs. More important, Franklin kept careful records of the weather in his part of the country during the eighteenth century. His records and those of other early meteorologists are a valuable help to modern scientists as they study weather patterns.

A January Fog Will Freeze a Hog is not only an old saying, but also the name of an excellent book about weather folklore by Hubert Davis (New York: Crown Publishers, 1977). **Read to find out** about other weather sayings. See if you can discover a scientific reason for each saying. Ask your grandparents or neighbors about weather folklore they have heard. Start your own collection of weather sayings—*your* grandchildren may ask you about them someday!

Name _____

A WEATHER LEGACY OF MY OWN

The Shepherd of Banbury lived in England over three hundred years ago. For decades he shared his weather observations with farmers and villagers as he travelled around the countryside with his sheep. Some of his weather predictors were published in *The Shepherd's Legacy* in 1670. People relied on them for many centuries, and scientists today confirm that much of his advice is accurate.

Try to make up sayings for some weather predictors that you have observed. Does your dog bark to come inside just before a thunderstorm? Have you noticed a strange yellow glow in the sky as a storm approaches? If a rainshower comes quickly and unexpectedly, does it usually pass over very quickly, too?

Use this page to begin a weather legacy of your own.

Name _____

WEATHER THAT MADE HISTORY

One thing that people have always recognized in weather is **change**. No one can be absolutely certain of tomorrow's sunshine. Sudden shifts in the weather have changed people's plans and the history of their communities since the beginning of time. Great floods, heavy snows, and roaring volcanoes are described in stories thousands of years old.

Natural weather disasters were often thought to be punishment from the gods. People tried to improve weather through magic, religious ceremonies, and rain dances. They held great celebrations to thank the gods for good weather.

When the powerful forces of Kublai Khan tried to invade Japan in the thirteenth century, the people fought bravely to keep the Mongols off their island. Just as supplies, weapons, and man power were running out, a tremendous monsoon stormed in from the Pacific and sank the invaders' entire fleet. The Japanese called the rainstorm **Kamikase** (wind from the gods) and celebrated its arrival.

Sometimes military leaders have worked in cooperation with the weather for the success of their campaign. Hannibal was prepared to cross the heavy snows of the Alps as he marched towards Rome hundreds of years ago. During the American Revolution, George Washington woke his troops in the middle of the night to take advantage of frozen roads that allowed them to move towards the British camps.

Even with the best preparations, weather has a mind of its own. During World War II, scientists worked hard to decide the best time for Allied troops to reach the Normandy beaches in France. They carefully studied the history of weather and tides along the coast, but the planned date of June 5, 1944, was stormier than usual. The invasion was delayed until June 6, and was successful despite continuing bad weather.

Although weather forecasting becomes more accurate every year, it is still a good idea to be ready to change plans when unpredictable weather strikes.

1. Early civilizations often blamed changes in the weather on
    a. natural atmospheric patterns.
    b. angry gods.
    c. the combination of sun, wind, and water.
2. If sudden rains had brought flooding to Texas during the Battle of the Alamo,
    a. it still would have turned out the same.
    b. the battle may have ended differently.
    c. the Texans would have won for sure.
3. When people say that weather has a "mind of its own," they probably mean
    a. that it thinks about what it's going to do tomorrow.
    b. that it acts without direction from man.
    c. that weather is easy to predict.

Name _____

STORIES ABOUT WEATHER AND PEOPLE

Think about weather and people. Choose one of the following ways to write about the relationship between unpredictable weather and the plans that people make.

1. Tell about a time when your own plans were changed because of the weather. What happened? How did you react to the change?
2. **Read to find out** how weather changed the course of history and any one particular event. (Sir Francis Drake, for example, was an English explorer who reached California in 1579 but couldn't find San Francisco Bay because of the heavy fog. Two centuries later the Spanish found the same coast and landed there!) Books about weather, like Life Science Library's *Weather* or Ingrid Holland's *Weather Facts and Feats* (Sterling Publishing Company, 1977) might be good places to start looking. Write about what you find out. Share it with your class.
3. Create your own story about people and weather. Imagine a friendly cloud that might help a young knight as he approaches a fiery dragon. Think about how a city street might look when the sun comes out to bring a special sparkle to buildings, sidewalks, and stoplights after a summer shower. How might the sudden sunshine affect a little boy who planned to go to the zoo with his aunt? Use your imagination! Tell how the weather makes people feel.

Name _____

PEOPLE CAN CHANGE THE WEATHER

It is easy to see that weather has always been a very basic concern of human life. Today people can make choices in planning for the weather with more reliability than ever before. Weather forecasts in the morning newspaper and on daily television programs are based on computer and satellite information **plus** human observation and experience. It is important to understand some of the factors that determine weather in order to best interpret the forecasts for our own immediate area.

Weather usually changes from week to week, season to season, based on the amount of heat from the **sun**, the **earth's shape and movement**, the **atmosphere**, and the particular **topography** (land and ocean features) of an area. Weather over a long period of time is called the **climate** of an area.

Sometimes people change the climate in a particular area through ignorance or accident. By building large cities, cutting down forests, constructing huge reservoirs, and filling in wetlands, people change the topography of their region. The heat from city areas and pollution produced in manufacturing can make drastic changes in atmosphere. Understanding more about weather can help people make choices based on sound ecological principles.

Scientists are learning to control the weather in small ways. Eventually they may be able to make positive changes like keeping a hurricane away from heavily populated areas or bringing water to people who are suffering from terrible droughts. Computers can help them to carefully calculate whether a change in one place might bring worse weather problems to another place. There are many things scientists still need to know before they can safely attempt major weather modifications. It is obvious that only through international cooperation could beneficial worldwide weather control be effective.

1. The way people use their natural resources (land, forests, water, air) affects the weather because
   a. weather is part of the earth's natural water cycle.
   b. trees depend on water for life.
   c. weather is caused by the sun alone.
2. People cause changes in the weather when they change
   a. the earth's shape and movement.
   b. the sun.
   c. the atmosphere and topography of an area.
3. From the article, it is easy to see that climate
   a. is found in wetland areas.
   b. never changes.
   c. is the weather in a particular area over a long period of time.

Name _____

SPINNING AROUND THE SUN

All life on earth depends on the sun, the huge, brilliant ball of fiery gases that radiates heat and light at the center of our universe. If the sun's heat were reduced by only 13 percent, scientists say that the entire earth would be covered with ice one mile thick. If the sun were 30 percent hotter, every bit of life would be broiled away.

As the earth travels around the sun 93 million miles away, three very basic facts affect weather in every part of the world.
1. The earth's orbit is elliptical. Sometimes it is much nearer to the sun than at other times.
2. The earth spins on its own axis. Parts of the earth face the sun during the day and turn away from the sun at night.
3. The earth is tilted so each hemisphere leans towards the sun during summer and away from the sun during winter.

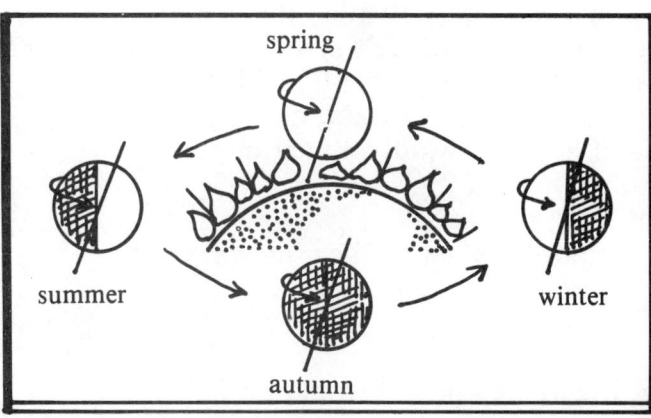

Two days each year are exactly as long as the night. They are called the **autumnal equinox**, (equal day and night) on September 22 and the **vernal equinox**, March 21. The sun crosses the equator on those days.

The shortest day of the year is always December 21, and the longest day of the year is June 21. These days are called **solstices**.

1. Day and night are caused by
   a. the elliptical orbit of the earth.
   b. the earth's spinning on its own axis.
   c. the earth's tilt as it travels around the sun.
2. If the earth were closer to the sun
   a. it would probably make temperatures more comfortable everywhere.
   b. water would probably evaporate and life would be cooked away.
   c. life on earth would continue just as it is.
3. The earth's relationship to the sun causes
   a. the longest and shortest days of the year.
   b. the weather and the seasons.
   c. both of the above.

Name _____

ATMOSPHERE

The earth's atmosphere is like an invisible glass dome that regulates the amount of the sun's rays that reach the land and seas. Without it, the sun's heat would be too much for the kinds of life found on our planet. Almost half of the sun's rays are turned back, but the rays that are absorbed stay with the earth longer because they can't pass out as easily as they come in. Scientists call this the **greenhouse effect**. It keeps the earth warm even at night and when the sun is hidden by clouds.

Solar rays that reach the earth are absorbed or reflected according to the surface they touch. New snow, for example, reflects almost 90 percent of the sun's rays. That's why snowy slopes do not melt under bright sunshine, and the skiers enjoying the mountains can get a sunburn despite chilly weather. Water absorbs the sun's rays if they come from directly overhead, but it reflects the rays if they bounce towards the wavy surface at an angle. Depending on how much radiation is reflected or absorbed, weather in an area varies.

All but one percent of the earth's atmosphere is in a layer only 19 miles thick, about as deep around the earth as the peel around an apple. The atmosphere's mixture of gases and water vapor weighs over 5600 trillion tons—a sea level pressure of 10 to 20 tons on every human being! Like the water it contains, air is constantly in a fluid, moving state. As it is heated by oceans or whirls over mountains, it becomes wind, another important weather factor.

1. The **greenhouse effect** keeps the earth warm at night because
    a. rays that pass into the earth's atmosphere cannot pass out of the atmosphere as easily.
    b. some sun is still shining at night.
    c. solar rays are reflected by many surfaces.
2. If there were no atmosphere around the earth, life as we know it would probably
    a. learn how to make atmosphere.
    b. not be able to exist because of the intense heat in the daytime and terrible cold at night.
    c. continue the same as it is now.
3. From these two articles it is possible to see that
    a. the sun and the atmosphere are two elements that make earth's weather.
    b. the earth's atmosphere is thousands of miles thick.
    c. the atmosphere reflects all of the sun's rays back into space.

Substances absorb different amounts of the sun's rays.

clouds 50%

lakes and oceans 70%

sand 30%   grass, dry soil 15%   forests, wet soil 10%   snow 70%

8

Name _____

WORLDWIDE AND LOCAL WINDS

When air is heated by the sun, it expands, becomes lighter, and rises. Cool air takes its place. This movement of the air is called **wind**. Unlike rain, snow, sunshine, or fog, you can't see the wind. It is an invisible force that must be measured by its effect on objects. When you look out a window, how can you tell if it's windy outside?

Think about the winds that you know. Have you ever felt a **draft** when wind squeezes through cracks in a door? Winds increase their speed to squeeze through mountains, between cliffs, across channels, and between tall buildings in big cities, too. A **gust** of wind is a quick increase in speed, and a **lull** is a decrease in the wind's average speed. **Turbulence** is the irregular motion of the wind up, down, and horizontally.

Large-scale, worldwide winds are caused by heat, by the shape and rotation of the earth, and are affected by the landforms or bodies of water over which you travel. Still, some worldwide winds are fairly predictable.

Since the sun is hottest at the Equator, most major winds start there. As the warm air rises, it moves towards the North and South Poles. As the air moves away from the Equator, it begins to cool down. Some of it returns to the Equator as **trade winds**, and some of it moves on towards the poles as **westerlies**.

Local winds are caused by the daily heating and cooling of the earth's surface in a particular area. Gentle breezes that come from a lake in midafternoon, or strong winds that whip along the slope of a mountain are examples of local winds. Turbulent weather is often produced when local and worldwide winds meet head on.

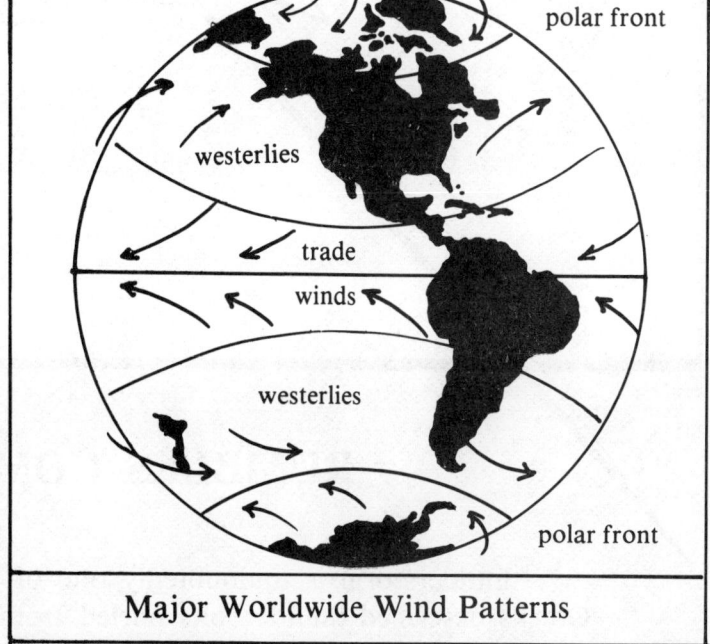
Major Worldwide Wind Patterns

Most of the wind that affects people is below a height of 30 feet. These **surface winds** are identified according to the compass point **from which** they blow. A SE (southeast) wind blows **from** the southeast **towards** the observer.

A **storm** is caused by rapidly moving warm air that can't mix with the icy cold air it meets. It forms a **front** of turbulent weather that may turn into a rainstorm, snowstorm, ice, sleet, hail, tornado, monsoon, or hurricane.

Name _____

RUMBLES COME TUMBLING!

A thunderstorm is undoubtedly one of nature's most awesome wonders. Ancient Greeks described thunderbolts hurled from angry gods at mankind. Chinese weather gods carried huge battle axes to tear apart trees, and flaming bolts of lightning to set fire to the earth. These early people were trying to explain a phenomenon (a circumstance or fact) in a way they could understand.

Do you remember what you used to think thunder was? Some modern stories imagine that thunder is the angels bowling or God moving his furniture around. These are lighthearted explanations usually told to small children in fun.

On a separate sheet of paper, write your own story to explain the shattering rumble of thunder and the flashes of lightning that dazzle in the skies during a violent thunderstorm. You may want to draw a picture to illustrate your story.

Can you think of some weather folklore for storms? Have you ever written a short poem to describe the way you feel during a thunderstorm? Put some of your own weather sayings, ideas, and feelings on the lines above.

10

Name _____

THUNDERSTORMS

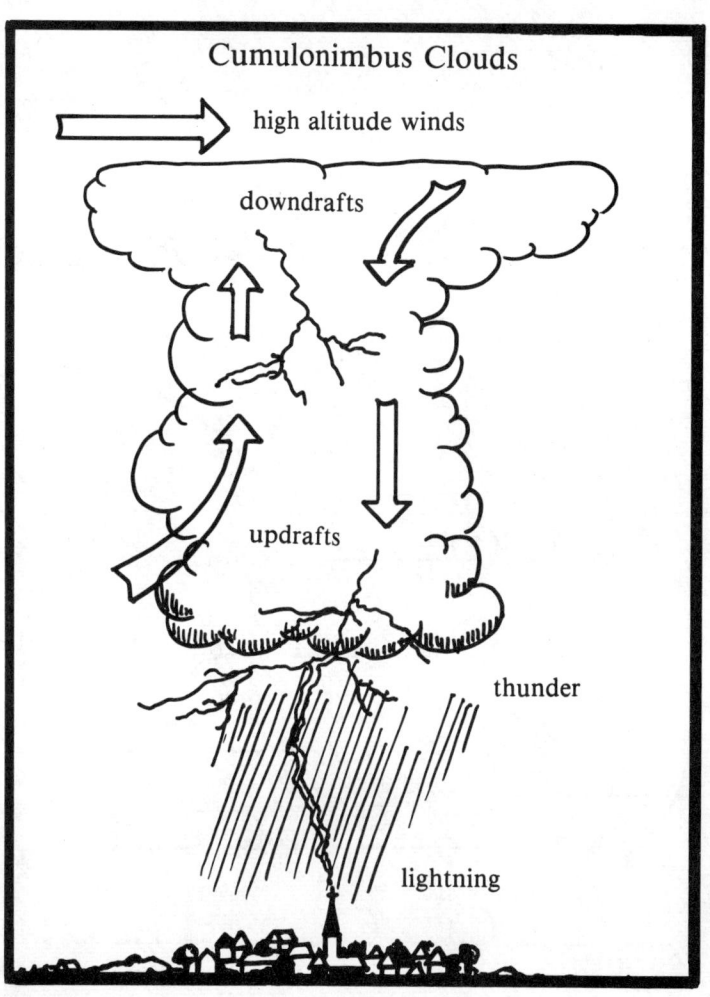

Thunderstorms are born in warm humid air when the atmosphere is unstable. A rising column of air produces white, billowing **cumulonimbus** clouds. Water vapor is changed into solid droplets. Inside the cloud, columns of air called **updrafts** continue to shoot higher. Sometimes these currents reach 60 miles per hour and travel as high as 60,000 feet.

Eventually, the growing cloud reaches stable layers of air. The top of the cloud flattens and spreads out. **Downdrafts** develop next to the rising air, and the cloud is filled with violent winds. Rain or hail begins to acquire enough weight to fall downward through the cloud to the earth.

Tremendous differences in electrical charge build up in cumulonimbus clouds as a result of friction, and the activity of supercooled water drops that freeze and splinter. The electricity is discharged as **lightning**. When a lightning flash heats the air, it violently expands to cause **thunder**.

Since light travels much faster than sound, it is possible to figure the distance of the lightning by measuring the seconds between flash and thunderclap. For each five seconds that pass, the lightning is about one mile away—sound travels at approximately one mile per five seconds.

Most thunderstorms only last about an hour. The cool air they bring is often welcome on a hot summer afternoon. Thunderstorm showers are helpful to forests and farms. Supercell thunderstorms along squall lines may last for longer periods and bring destructive wind gusts, continuous lightning, hail, and even tornadoes. **Hailstones** can easily damage crops, bringing tremendous economic loss.

A thunderstorm's combination of wind, turbulence (rapidly churning updrafts and downdrafts), lightning, and hail can cause particular problems for aircraft. Icing can occur on airplane wings when they travel through supercooled clouds.

Name _____

A SUPERCOOLED PUZZLE

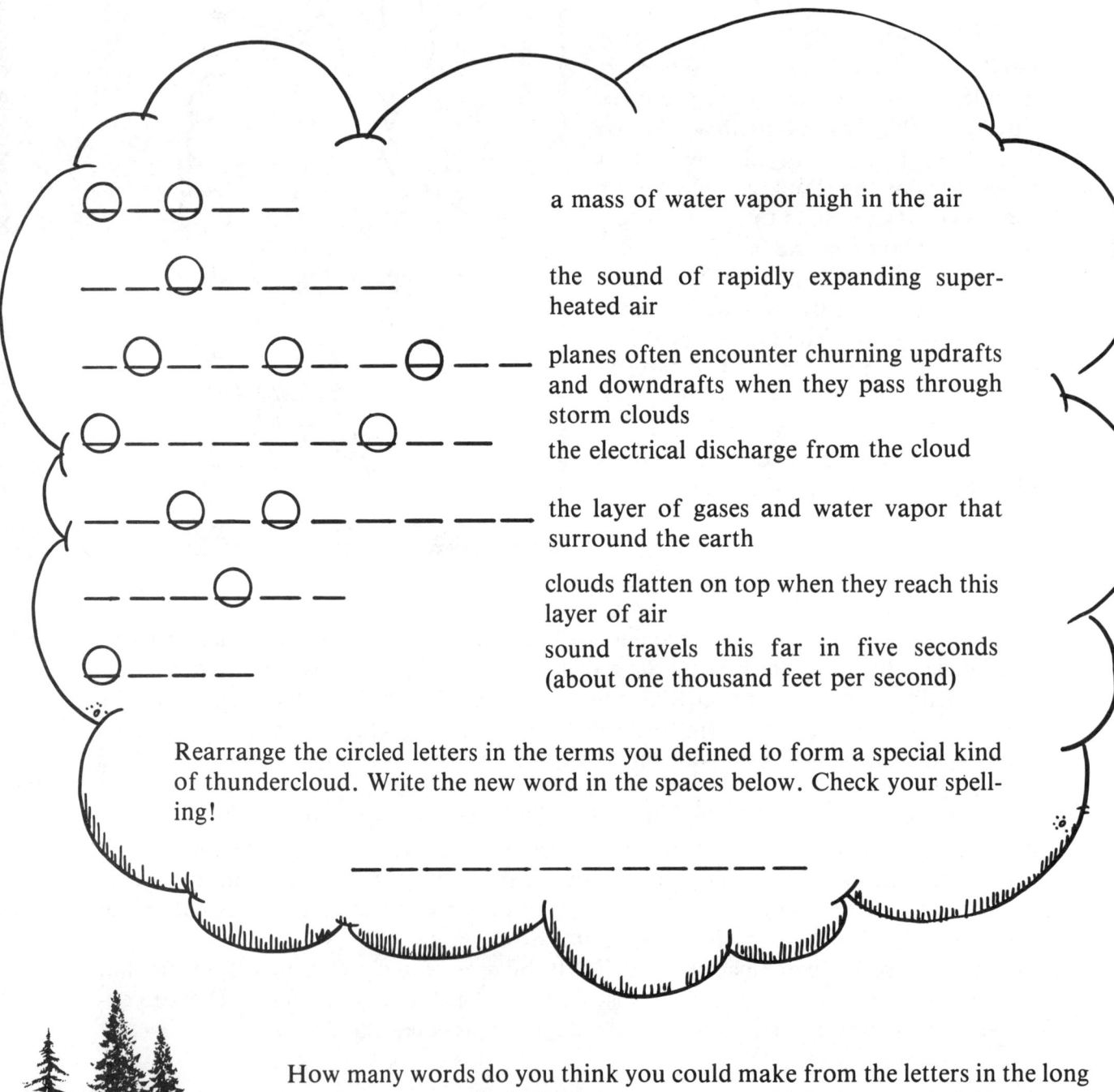

Ⓞ_Ⓞ_ _ _   a mass of water vapor high in the air

_ _Ⓞ_ _ _ _ _   the sound of rapidly expanding super-heated air

_Ⓞ_ _ _Ⓞ_ _Ⓞ_ _   planes often encounter churning updrafts and downdrafts when they pass through storm clouds

Ⓞ_ _ _ _ _Ⓞ_ _ _   the electrical discharge from the cloud

_ _Ⓞ_Ⓞ_ _ _ _ _ _   the layer of gases and water vapor that surround the earth

_ _ _Ⓞ_ _   clouds flatten on top when they reach this layer of air

Ⓞ_ _ _   sound travels this far in five seconds (about one thousand feet per second)

Rearrange the circled letters in the terms you defined to form a special kind of thundercloud. Write the new word in the spaces below. Check your spelling!

_ _ _ _ _ _ _ _ _ _ _ _ _

How many words do you think you could make from the letters in the long word you just spelled? Write how many you think you can find. Rearrange the letters any way you want, but only use the letters in the word.

I think I can find _____ words.

Now try it! What letters are missing that might have helped you find more words?

Name _____

LIGHTNING

Hector Berlioz's *Fantastic Symphony* beautifully recreates the majesty of rumbling thunder. In *The Grand Canyon Suite*, Ferde Grofé includes the sounds of a tremendous storm. Paintings and photographs often show lightning as it illuminates the horizon with its forked river of brilliance. People have always been struck by the dazzling power of a thunderstorm.

There are actually two parts to every lightning flash. **Leader strokes** are often invisible as they dart from cloud to cloud. Eventually they leave the cloud base looking for a clear channel to the tallest objects on the ground. When the final leader stroke reaches the ground, the **return stroke** flashes back up the channel to light up the sky. The return strokes are much brighter and faster than the leaders.

Lightning only lasts a millionth of a second, but the image on the human eye or camera lens remains for a while longer. The damage it causes can be permanent.

Even though only 20 percent of the lightning in a thunderstorm actually reaches the ground, it is enough to cause over 9000 forest fires every year in the United States. Miles of valuable timberland are destroyed. Wildlife and recreational facilities disappear. It takes a long time for a forest to renew itself after a major fire.

1. The brilliant flash that we usually call lightning is actually the
   a. leader stroke.
   b. return stroke.
   c. vaporization.
2. Trees and forests are often struck by lightning because
   a. thunderstorms form over trees.
   b. leader strokes of lightning look for the tallest objects in the area.
   c. wood attracts lightning.
3. From this article, it is easy to see that
   a. lightning is as powerful a force as people have always thought.
   b. most of the lightning in a storm reaches the ground.
   c. forest fires are rarely caused by lightning.

Name _____

LIGHTNING SAFETY PRECAUTIONS

Ten thousand thunderstorms occur every day as part of the earth's natural water cycle. While they never occur in the polar regions, some areas have hundreds of thunderstorm days each year. In Java, Indonesia, the mountain city of Bogor has over three hundred thunderstorm days a year!

Considering that about 2000 thunderstorms are taking place right now somewhere in the world, it is not surprising that at least one person a day is struck by lightning. In the United States, about 200 people are killed by lightning every year. Many others are hurt by lightning but survive. Your chances of getting hit by lightning are much less than the chances of getting killed in a traffic accident, yet it is a much more common occurrence than being caught in a tornado or hurricane.

You can reduce the risk even more by following some clear safety rules during a thunderstorm. Remember that water and metal are powerful conductors of electricity.

1. **NEVER** stay in a swimming pool, on a beach, golf course or open field when a thunderstorm is approaching. **Even if it sounds far away, don't take any chances!**
2. If you are outside, try to get into a house or large building. A car is safer than being outside; a clump of low trees might provide some protection. **NEVER** stand under a tall tree. **Lightning is always attracted to the tallest object in an area.** Don't stay in a boat, on a hilltop, or near anything made of metal. If you're caught in a field, crouch low to the ground. Don't lie flat.
3. If you are inside, it's a good idea to stay away from windows, water faucets, sinks, tubs, and the telephone. Don't use toasters, irons, or anything that could carry electricity if it were to strike wires near your house.

1. Lightning is especially dangerous to golfers because
   a. they don't see the storm coming.
   b. they don't hear the storm coming.
   c. they are often a long distance from the nearest shelter and are often the tallest object around.
2. If you're swimming when you hear thunder in the distance, it's a good idea to
   a. wait awhile before calling it a day.
   b. get out of the water right away.
   c. watch for the storm to get closer.
3. From this article it is easy to see that
   a. there are ways to protect yourself from the dangers of electrical storms.
   b. you can make lots of phone calls when you're stuck inside during a thunderstorm.
   c. thunderstorms are very rare.

Name _____

INSIDE A THUNDERSTORM

William H. Rankin was a Marine Corps pilot who learned more about thunderstorms by accident than most people could discover in a lifetime of study. He was flying over South Carolina in 1960 when the power went out in his airplane. It began to dive toward a huge, black thundercloud nearly one hundred miles wide. He ejected from the plane and began to parachute towards the earth. He fell right into the middle of the thundercloud!

Major Rankin described being thrown around by winds while blinding flashes of red hot light blazed on all sides of him. His parachute collapsed over him and tangled around his legs. He fell towards a huge, black hole; then suddenly he was thrown upwards by a crashing, roaring gush of wind. Rain was pouring around him so heavily that he compared it with being under a waterfall. When he breathed, water filled his nose and mouth. Many times he thought he would lose consciousness from the battering wind and deafening roar of thunder that shook his whole body. When Major Rankin finally fell below the storm, his parachute opened and he reached the ground.

What should have been a ten-minute fall took William Rankin over forty minutes! His story is told in the Houghton Mifflin reading series in an article called "The Man Who Fell Up." Scientists and meteorologists have studied Rankin's description carefully for more clues to the nature of the thunderstorm.

1. William H. Rankin's parachute jump took forty minutes because
    a. he was very high above the clouds.
    b. he was often thrown across the clouds and back up into the storm by the violent winds and air masses in the thunderhead.
    c. his parachute opened slowly and got caught around his legs.
2. It was probably lucky that Major Rankin's parachute closed around him termporarily because
    a. if it remained open it may have been ripped apart in the twisting wind and rain.
    b. it made him fall more slowly.
    c. it provided protection from the rain.
3. Major Rankin's experience helps scientists understand
    a. the tremendous forces taking place inside the thundercloud.
    b. how pilots react to parachuting from airplanes.
    c. accurate ways to predict the arrival of thunderstorms.

Name _____

SOME COLD, HARD FACTS

The earth is sometimes called the Water Planet. Much more of its water is in the form of ice and snow than most people think. One-tenth of the world is covered with a **permanent ice sheet** as much as three miles thick! In Greenland and Antarctica, an area the size of the United States and Europe together is covered with ice—over 5,700,000 square miles. If the ice were to melt, the level of the oceans would rise over 250 feet.

The coldest permanently inhabited place in the world is the village of Oymyakon in Siberia, USSR. Temperatures of -96° F have been recorded over the permanently frozen ground in Oymyakon. At the South Pole, average July temperatures are -130° F. Sometimes temperatures in a particular place can vary a great deal in a single day. In Browning, Montana, on January 23, 1916, temperatures dropped from 44° F to -56° F during a 24-hour period!

Ice in the Arctic and Antarctic Circles reflects heat back into space, so very few clouds form at the Poles. Snow rarely falls in these areas. World record snowfalls are all in the United States. The Rocky Mountains average 300-400 inches of snow every winter. In 1972, Mt. Rainier, Washington, recorded over 102 feet of snow!

Snowflakes usually land at a speed of only 3-5 feet per second. One inch of rain has about the same amount of water as one foot of snow. People in Bratsk, Siberia, reported snowflakes 8'' x 12'' large in 1971. Sometimes water falls as rain or **sleet**, then freezes on contact with the ground or exposed objects. In an ice storm, an evergreen tree 50 feet high and 20 feet wide can be covered with over five tons of ice!

For thousands of years, people have recognized the value of cold as a preservative. Bacteria cannot survive in extreme cold, so materials stay exactly as they are without decaying. Communities used the cold to keep meats fresh through long, icy winters. Less than a hundred years ago scientists discovered a way to make this kind of refrigeration artificially.

People have found mammoth elephants perserved in glaciers thousands of years old. Grasses from the elephant's last meal were perfectly perserved on his tusks!

Ancient Romans made **ice cream** from snow blocks carried down from the mountains. Igloos made from ice and snow have a unique construction that cannot be duplicated with any other materials. These houses keep Eskimo families warm and cozy in the winter.

16

Name _____

BERGY BITS AND GROWLERS

    Bergy bits and **growlers** might sound like something on the menu at the All-American Hot Dog Stand, but they are actually scientific terms that climatologists use to describe icebergs.
    Here is a list of some other important and interesting winter weather terminology. See if you can add to it as you study snow and ice through this unit. **Read to find out** more about the causes and consequences of each term.
    Hailstones are ice crystals that are tossed about in cumulonimbus clouds until they are heavily coated with ice sheets in rings. They are usually about the size of marbles when they fall to the ground and can greatly damage crops. Two boys in Kansas found a soccer ball-sized hailstone weighing almost two pounds in 1970!
    Graupel is a German word for soft hail which is really snow that has partly melted and refrozen, then falls to the ground as thin ice pellets.
    Dry snow is very cold crystals that skiers call powder snow. It doesn't melt together or form snowballs easily.
    Wet snow makes perfect snowballs! It compacts easily and stays frozen longer.
    Glaciers are huge sheets of ice formed over centuries by snow that compresses and doesn't even melt. Over 6 million square miles of the earth's surface is covered by glaciers! They move slowly but constantly, cutting away huge mountains, and sculpturing new peaks and valleys in the earth.
    Ice shelves sometimes three miles thick float over the North and South Poles.
    Icebergs are broken sections of glaciers or of the ice shelf. Nine-tenths of the iceberg is usually under water.
    Permafrost is permanently frozen land. In Canada, about half the land is permanently frozen. In Siberia, a very cold part of Russia, the permafrost is almost a mile deep.
    Avalanche is a whole layer of snow breaking away from a mountainside and tumbling with great speed into a valley. Tremendous winds that build up ahead of an avalanche can blow houses apart before the snow reaches them. European Alps sometimes have disastrous avalanches in the spring when parts of the snow begin to melt.
Read to find out about clouds, cyclones, fogs, dry ice, artificial snow, frost, the greenhouse effect, cryogenics, ice crystals, the Matterhorn, sea surges, monsoons, rime, snow-eater winds, mirages, the Brocken Spectre, the aurora borealis, water devils, and wind vanes. There's so much to know about weather!

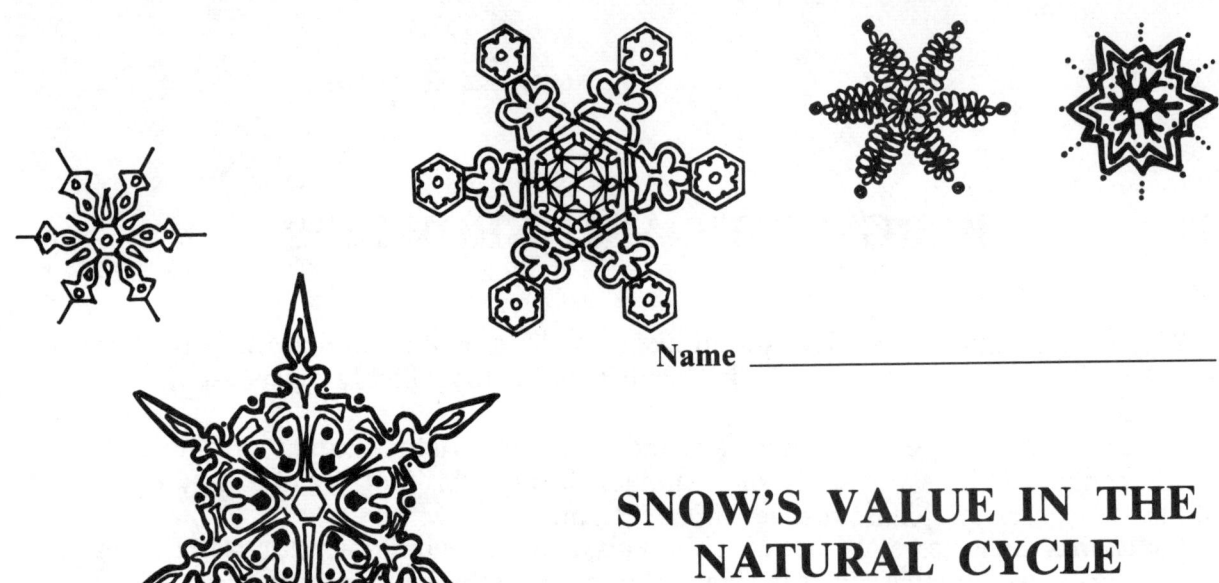

Name _____

SNOW'S VALUE IN THE NATURAL CYCLE

Snow is a natural and valuable part of the world's water cycle. A loosely packed layer of snow is full of air. Like thermal underwear for the earth, the air trapped in snow keeps the cold winds out and the warmer air in. Animals who don't have winter nests often burrow in the snow for protection from the cold. Sleeping plant life and root systems are protected, too. Bulbs and seeds often germinate and begin to grow beneath the gentle snow.

Some flowers, like the edelweiss, only grow high in the snowy Alps. Animals like the polar bear and the penguin would miss the snow and find it difficult to survive without its protection and life-giving habitat.

When snow melts slowly, water is easily absorbed into the ground. Farmers appreciate this natural irrigation for winter crops and for preparing the ground for spring planting.

Powdery snow acts like millions of ball bearings for the eager, experienced skier. Snowmobiles glide across acres of snowy fields and hills, and children look forward to winter sports like sledding, ice skating, and toboggan racing.

1. The farmers of the world appreciate snow when it
    a. melts slowly to provide a natural water supply for their crops.
    b. provides beautiful scenery for photographing and painting.
    c. gives them a winter off work.
2. Snow is a special protection for the polar bear because
    a. it keeps him warm.
    b. it matches his natural color and allows him to be camouflaged.
    c. it covers his fishing holes on the ice.
3. From this article, it is easy to see that
    a. snow is dangerous and harmful to all plant and animal life.
    b. snow is a natural and valuable part of the earth's water cycle.
    c. snow is never fun for people.

Name _____

SCIENTIFIC ROOT WORDS

The meaning and pronunciation of many scientific words are easy to figure out if you know a few basic **root words**. It's a good idea to learn as many Latin and Greek root words as you can. Make a collection of them to share with your classmates!

The root **-graph**, for example, means **picture** or **illustration**. The root **phono-** means **sound**. Together these two roots make the word **phonograph** which means **picture made of sound**. That's the music that comes from stereos (but stereo- means something else! Can you find out what the root word means?)

How many other words can you make with phono- or -graph in them?

_____   _____

_____   _____

_____   _____

_____

Sometimes you can use creative thinking to discover the meanings of new words by breaking them into parts and associating the parts with words you already know. On the next page you will read about **photomicrographs**. Write the three root words that make the word **photomicrograph**.

_____   _____   _____

Now think of some other words that contain each of these word parts. What do you think **photomicrograph** might mean? Write a short definition below.

_____

_____

Read to find out if your idea was accurate. Here are some other common root words that are often used in scientific descriptions of snow, blizzards, thunderstorms, and other natural phenomena. See if you can find their meanings.

hydro-	alti-	-logy	-meter	trans-
-trope	terra-	infra-	bio-	-sphere
strato-	electro-	thermo-	-trophe	hypo-

Why do you think some root words are written with a hyphen (-) before and after each part? What could this tell you about where the word part might be located in the complete word?

Name _____

WILLIAM BENTLEY AND THE SNOWFLAKE

William A. Bentley (1865-1931) was a teenager working on his father's farm when his interest in snowflakes began. He was delighted with the natural beauty, artistic form, and scientific precision of each individual snowflake. He decided to collect snowflakes the best way he could.

Although the art of photomicrography was only beginning, William carefully fit a camera to a microscope. He experimented with lighting and background. Soon he started to collect excellent examples of snow crystals.

While he continued to farm, William Bentley spent forty years developing a set of over 6000 photomicrographs of snowflakes. Each one was different! A book called *Snow Crystal* was published just before William died. It contained 2000 of his best photographs.

From Bentley's collection and other scientific investigations, experts have been able to study the formation, growth, and specific types of snowflakes. They have been able to group snowflakes into eight main types.

1. William A. Bentley began to collect snowflakes because
   a. he was interested in their design and beauty.
   b. it helped him to be a better farmer.
   c. there were excellent photomicrographic techniques available.
2. Bentley was able to develop his collection because
   a. people paid him highly for it.
   b. he patiently stuck with his photographing through many years.
   c. it was his job.
   3. From this article, it is easy to see that
      a. snowflakes are really very much alike.
      b. no one knows how many kinds of snowflakes there are.
      c. one person can make a tremendous contribution during his lifetime.

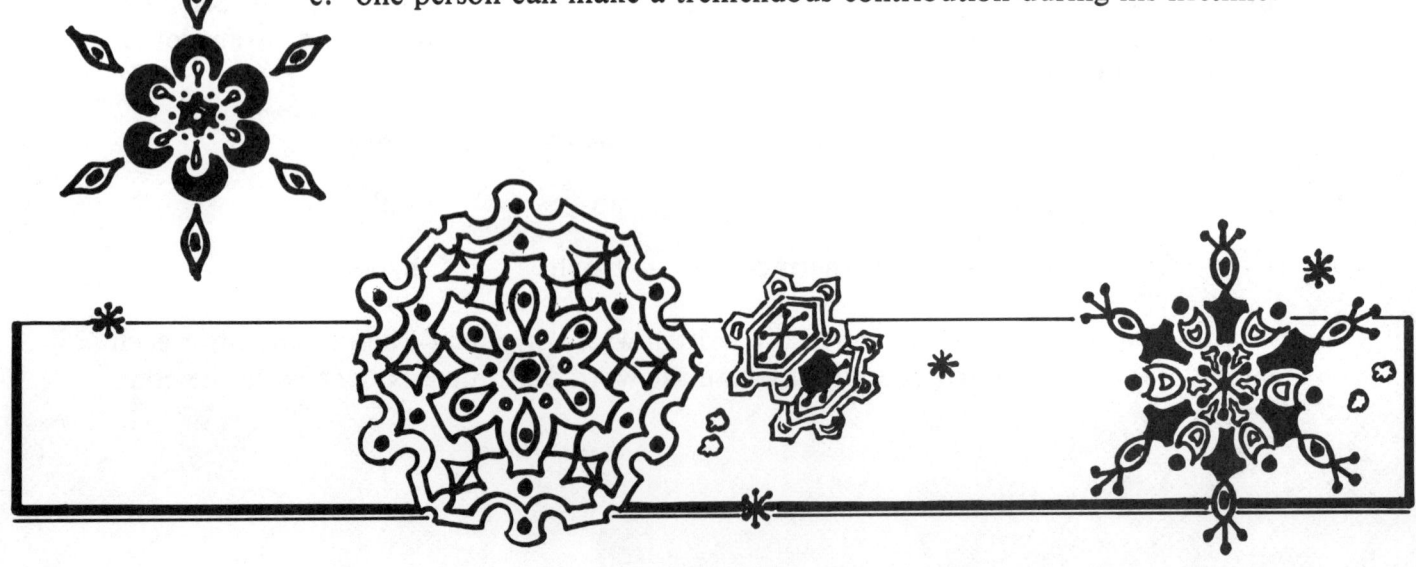

Name _____

SNOWFLAKES

Stellar snowflakes are six-sided star flakes, the most familiar kind of snowflake.

Hexagonal (six-sided) **plates** are thin solid ice crystals.

Graupel is a German word for the soft-clumped flakes that are coated wth frozen water droplets.

Hexagonal columns are six-sided prisms of ice, the simplest kind of snowflake. Experts say that most snowflakes begin as columns in the clouds.

Capped hexagonal columns have a plate of perfectly shaped ice crystals at each end and sometimes in the middle of the column.

Ice needles are very tiny columns with sharp ends. Sometimes they have small branches.

Powder snow is made up of tiny ice crystals too small and dry to have a particular shape. These flakes rarely clump together.

Asymmetrical crystals do not have the balanced shape and beautiful design of hexagonal flakes. They may be broken bits that have clumped together, or wind and pressure in the clouds may have interrupted their growth. They have irregular, unusual shapes.

If you live in an area that has snowy winter weather, make a snowflake collection of your own! You can catch them on cold pieces of dark construction paper, or any mitten will do!

Practice identifying the types of snowflakes on these pages.

A. _____ F. _____
B. _____ G. _____
C. _____ H. _____
D. _____ I. _____
E. _____ J. _____

21

Name _____

MORE TEACHER IDEAS!
ADDED DIMENSIONS

A class discussion like "Some Cold, Hard Facts" (p. 16) helps broaden children's understanding of snow and its impact on the land and its people. Depending on their experience, many students may have previously thought of snow from a limited perspective—perhaps their own personal enjoyment of it on vacations, perhaps the inconveniences it may have caused them in the past.

Challenge students to discover their own **snow facts**. Suggest resources for researching the **coldest, snowiest, shortest, iciest** days in your own region. Interested students might want to compare their records with nearby areas that are quite different. If mountains, lakes, or other topographical influences have affected the weather in your area, challenge children to explore the reasons behind these weather changes.

Even children who live in a geographical area that has little or no winter weather extremes enjoy sharing snow stories about treasured personal memories of snow at Grandma's or on vacation. Make a snow booklet for the reading corner with their written and illustrated narratives. Share them orally as time permits.

Snow by Isao Sasaki and *The Cat on the Dovrefell* illustrated by Tomie de Paola are easy reading picture books that students through sixth grade enjoy. There are beautifully photographed snow books like Phyllis Busch's *A Walk in the Snow*. Ask children to bring in winter books that they have found and enjoyed. Be sure to share "Stopping by Woods on a Snowy Evening" by Robert Frost and other winter poetry.

To extend children's understanding of snow, there are excellent science investigations that illustate frost, dew, condensation, and crystals. For creative experiences, Good Apple's *Winter Wonders* includes dozens of activities for even the youngest children.

Name _____

DESIGNS IN A WINTER MOTIF

A fresh cover of snow provides a peaceful, beautiful natural scene that artists have captured in paintings and photographs throughout the years. Mountain villages high above the snowy valleys are settings for favorite stories like *Heidi* and true stories like *The Sound of Music*. *Hans Brinker and the Silver Skates* is a children's classic from Holland, and all ages enjoy *The Snow Queen*, one of Hans Christian Andersen's beloved fairy tales from Denmark.

Children have a chance to **think snow** while they create original and unique expressions of winter themes in "Designs in a Winter Motif," a classroom activity from Good Apple's *Times to Treasure*.

Introduce children to the notion of *motif* through everyday examples from wallpaper, material, and music (like the soundtracks from *Close Encounters*, *Rocky*, or *Jaws*). A repeated design, theme, phrase or pattern can make a house "early American" or a building "Greek." It conveys a mood or a message in music and art.

Seasons have a motif, too. Some designs particularly belonging to winter might be Jack Frost, snowmen, frozen ponds, hot chocolate, and warm fireplaces. Ski trails, snow-covered villages, bare trees, and warm mittens are other winter motifs. What about cold noses, shovels, skates, and sleds?

Have children divide a piece of 8 x 10 art paper into random (another learning experience!) geometric spaces with five straight lines. Decide on a winter theme. Each child can draw his main design in a space on his paper. Then he chooses parts of his dominant theme to enlarge or miniaturize for other spaces. Just a color from the design might be repeated in an area or a button, snowflake or smile.

"Designs in a Winter Motif" are a natural delight for children. Their innate sense of balance and rhythm is a wonder in itself! Let them experiment. Encourage them to be bold and to be themselves.

The finished designs make an unusual border display for the winter classroom or the science area where students are studying winter storms and blizzards.

Name _____

WINTER SURVIVAL: MIGRATION AND HIBERNATION

Almost all living creatures need food, water, and warmth to survive. Winter brings less food, frozen water, and cold, so animals must move to warmer climates or adapt to winter conditions in order to live.

Those who move are called *migratory* animals. Except for Santa's crew, reindeer migrate from polar regions to warmer southern climates each year. The Arctic tern is a tiny bird that breeds at the North Pole, then travels 29,000 miles round trip to Australia or Antarctica every year in its migratory pattern. Millions of monarch butterflies travel together from the northern states to Florida and Texas, then return to the north in the summer. People spent thousands of years migrating to more hospitable climates around the world.

Some animals that stay in the cold regions *hibernate* through the winter to conserve energy. Their temperatures drop, and all bodily functions slow down. Dormice, hedgehogs, and bats don't need food when they hibernate, and their warm nests keep them from freezing. Bears don't really hibernate, but spend long sleepy winters wrapped in heavy protective layers of fat. Snakes and insects are cold-blooded creatures that sleep in the ground below the frostline during the winter. Scientists wonder about the possibility of adopting hibernation as a way to help people travel long distances in space explorations.

1. Some animals and birds migrate each year because
    a. they like to travel and see new places.
    b. they need warmer climates in order to survive.
    c. this builds up an extra layer of fat to protect them from the cold.
2. If people could hibernate for long periods during space travel, they
    a. wouldn't need as much food or supplies to survive.
    b. would get to their destinations faster.
    c. couldn't go as far.
3. From this article, we can see that
    a. many creatures don't need food or water to survive.
    b. migration and hibernation are two ways the creatures survive cold winters.
    c. all animals have learned to live in the cold.

24

Name _____

ADAPTING TO WINTER CLIMATES

Some animals adapt to cold weather through body changes that help them to survive during long and severe winters. The Arctic fox has shorter ears and muzzles than other foxes to cut down heat loss. Its fur turns white and grows much longer in the winter. The snowshoe rabbit and polar bear have thick, hairy footpads that act as snowshoes when they travel across snow and ice. The whale, seal, and walrus all have tremendous stores of fatty tissue to protect them from the cold. Thirty tons of the seventy-ton whale is blubber. Insects at the North Pole are black to absorb the sun's heat, and many have glycerol in their blood to keep it from freezing.

People who live in the Arctic eat very rich, fatty foods so their bodies can adapt to the cold. In addition, they have learned to build unique, warm houses from the ice and snow. Their igloos protect them against severe wind and storms.

1. The Indians who live in the Andes Mountains in South America, the highest inhabited area in the world, have round, barrel-like chests that enable them to breathe rapid, shallow breaths in air that has little oxygen. Their bodies have
   a. adapted to their environment so they can survive.
   b. nothing to do with their survival.
   c. made it harder for them to live in the mountains.
2. Identify the examples that show how people can bring their own weather with them to unusual environments.
   a. Scientists who spend months deep in the ocean bring oxygen and fresh water supplies with them in their submarines.
   b. Astronauts wear space suits on the moon.
   c. Weather stations in Antarctica have food flown in to their specially equipped and constructed communities.
3. From this article, it is easy to see that people
   a. have difficulty adapting to their environment.
   b. plan many ways to survive in cold or strange climates.
   c. must always move away from the cold.

Name _____

WINTER STORMS: CAUSE AND EFFECTS

When *cold polar air* and *warm tropical air masses* meet, there is a turbulence as the fronts try to balance themselves. Low pressure systems bring violent storms, snow, and hail. High winds keep the snow from settling, and blizzards rage over hundreds of miles.

In some parts of the United States, winter storms are expected. East of the Colorado Rockies, storms move across the plains towards the Great Lakes. Disturbances over the Gulf of Mexico move north across the Midwest. Winter storms that form along the coast of Virginia and the Carolinas move up the Atlantic seaboard towards Greenland.

Wherever they strike, winter storms bring particular devastation. When they move on, the cold air causes heavy snows and ice to remain for a long time. Sometimes the storms cause loss of life and property. They always cause inconvenience and disruption of normal routines. People in rural areas are often isolated. Crops are sometimes destroyed for the whole year. Livestock must be protected. Economic losses can be staggering. Traffic and communication in larger cities are often brought to a standstill.

1. Winter storms can be particularly disastrous because
    a. the heavy snows and ice cause problems a long time after the actual storm is over.
    b. they keep people from enjoying the outdoors.
    c. they come so unexpectedly.
2. To prepare for blizzards, people who own livestock can
    a. provide shelter for cattle and haul extra feed to feeding areas before the storm arrives.
    b. hope the storm passes over quickly.
    c. let the cattle try to make it on their own.
3. From this article we can see that winter storms usually
    a. strike anywhere at any time.
    b. are very mild and cause little difficulty.
    c. follow particular patterns and can be expected in some parts of the country every year.

Name _____

READY OR NOT, HERE I COME!

    People who settle in cities located in climates that get very cold must plan to adapt to winter conditions. Communities in the mountains and northern United States have learned to expect heavy snows and bitter cold in the winter. Their houses are built to protect them from the weather. Storm windows are double paned to provide an insulating layer of air. The roof is steeply slanted and reinforced so heavy snows cause less damage. People have shovels, sand, and snowblowers ready to clear driveways and sidewalks. Heating systems are designed for cold weather, and wood stoves or fireplaces add extra warming possibilities.

    In areas rarely affected by severe winters, people are much less prepared for them. In January, 1973, a devastating ice storm with sleet and heavy snow crippled cities in Georgia, South Carolina, and North Carolina. The states had little or no emergency snow equipment or supplies. Water and fuel pipes that were not reinforced froze and burst. Homes and buildings were not insulated for great cold, and power lines were not able to support heavy icing. Crops were killed and many orchards and farms were permanently damaged. Communication and transportation stopped. It was weeks before the city of Atlanta was able to resume business as usual.

1. Winter storms in the South are particularly catastropic because
   a. the ice is heavy and thick.
   b. people are not prepared to cope with them.
   c. they come very often.
2. During severe icy weather in the South, expressways and airports probably
   a. operate as usual.
   b. experience a little delay.
   c. close completely.
3. It is easy to see from this article that
   a. winter storms never strike unexpectedly.
   b. preparation is good protection during winter weather.
   c. it is impossible for cold winter weather to strike the South.

Name _____

MONITORING WORLDWIDE WEATHER

A weather forecast is a prediction of coming weather. The forecast is based on reports from observers at sea, on the ground, and in the air. The forecast is only as accurate as the information that has been gathered, so weather forecasters try to collect tremendous amounts of carefully measured data.

Ground weather stations report temperatures, pressure, clouds, winds, humidity and rainfall from points around the world. Nations cooperate to pass along information through the **World Meteorological Association**. Weather balloons are sent thousands of feet up to transmit atmospheric data to the meteorological stations below. Ships and airplanes take regular weather readings to relay to international bureaus.

All of this information is compared with the history of weather in particular areas. Hundreds of mathematical computations can be done in minutes with the help of modern computers. As the incoming information is adjusted continually, the computers work to adjust and perfect the forecasts.

Today's scientists rely on satellites that can effectively read ocean temperatures to a depth of over 25 feet and atmospheric temperatures of a height of over 100,000 feet. Factors at both of these extremes affect weather for any one area. Millions of pieces of data are measured by satellites every day, and computations are carefully studied to help make forecasts that are valuable to farmers, pilots, fishermen, highway construction crews, truckers, vacation resorts, businessmen, and fifth graders planning field trips.

1. Satellites are particularly valuable in weather forecasting because
   a. they can measure temperatures high in the atmosphere and below sea level.
   b. observations from machines have replaced observations from people.
   c. they move across weather fronts very slowly.
2. Tremendous amounts of information probably
   a. add up to more accurate weather forecasting.
   b. confuse the scientists.
   c. are not available.
3. From this article it is easy to see that weather forecasting
   a. is really just individual guesses.
   b. has nothing to do with weather in an area that has happened in the past.
   c. is more accurate than ever as human observation is combined with satellite information, history, and computer calculations.

Name _____

SNOW AND MORE SNOW

The National Weather Service uses seven different degrees of snowfall to warn people about approaching storms. If people know these snow terms, they can understand more from weather reports on radio and television.

Snow flurries are snowfalls that only last a short while, may reduce visibility as they fall, and don't usually build up much snow on the ground.

Snow squalls are very intense, brief snowfalls usually accompanied by gusty winds.

Snow means that the snowfall will probably last for several hours with snow accumulating on the ground.

Blowing and drifting snow occur when strong winds lift falling snow and surface snow that it is blown around in the air. Visibility is greatly reduced.

Drifting snow is used in weather forecasts when snow on the ground will probably be blown around into huge drifts against objects standing in its path.

Ground blizzard is drifting snow, especially on the northern plains, that blows so much that it is like another snowfall.

Blizzards carry strong winds, huge amounts of snow, and severe cold that are often disastrous for people and animals.

Anyone who has left the door open for even a minute in icy weather knows how to change warm to cold (and how Mom shouts at him to close the door). See if you can change **warm** to **cold** by changing only one letter of each word at a time. The first one is done for you. Is there more than one way to change warm to cold?

```
W A R M
W O R M
_ _ _ _

_ _ _ _
C O L D
```

Changing **rain** to **hail** is easy. Try it! How many steps does it take to change **rain** to **snow**? See if you can think of other weather words to challenge your friends. Do you think all words could eventually be changed from one to another if they have the same number of letters? Why or why not?

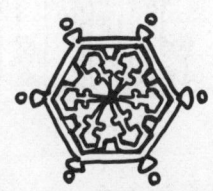

29

Name _____

COLD AMERICAN WINTERS

Blizzards are particularly dangerous winter storms that can totally immobilize even the largest, well-prepared cities. Snowfall is heavy and constant, often lasting many days. The blizzard is accompanied by tremendous winds that keep the snow from settling. Huge drifts can eventually bury cars and houses. It is impossible to see even a few feet ahead in a blizzard. Animals or people caught outside have no way to find shelter.

A combination of severe winds, extreme cold, and heavy snow paralyzed the United States east of the Rocky Mountains in late January, 1977. Temperatures set record lows in 19 states. In Buffalo, New York, 76 mile-per-hour winds blew six feet of snow into solid, rock-hard drifts 30 feet high. More snow fell, covering houses and buildings. Weeks later when the blizzards eased, the low temperatures continued. Tons of icy snow were loaded on trains to be shipped out of the city. Through the winter, over 200 inches of snow fell on Buffalo.

Meanwhile, a violent storm rocked the Great Lakes region with blizzard after blizzard. Along the New England coast, 82 mile-per-hour winds caused huge waves. Tides flooded the cities, winds broke seawalls with waves that tore into homes and destroyed beaches. Then two feet of snow covered the devastated areas.

During the winter of 1984-85, another series of disastrous winter blizzards and icy weather claimed hundreds of lives in the eastern half of the United States. Over one billion dollars in Florida crop damage was caused by the Arctic storm nicknamed the Alberta Clipper. At the same time, record snows and low temperatures rocked Europe from England and Germany as far southward as the Italian coast and the French Riviera. Snow fell in Rome for the first time in nearly two decades, and many areas recorded their lowest temperatures in over thirty years.

1. Blizzards are a combination of
   a. rain and hail.
   b. ice and frost.
   c. icy weather, snow, and wind.
2. The people of Buffalo probably removed their snow by railroad because
   a. the city was already clogged with much more snow than it could handle.
   b. it was the easiest way to get rid of it.
   c. it was melting very rapidly.
3. On the New England coast, destruction was caused by
   a. snow alone.
   b. too much ice.
   c. tides, winds, waves, and snow.

Name _____

THE STORY OF SNOW AT DONNER PASS

Early American settlers struggled with loneliness, long days of difficult travels, Indians, lack of supplies, and sickness, but some of their worst hardships were often caused by weather. Their wagons were stopped by mud during heavy rains, their cattle and horses died from lack of water on desert plains and during droughts, their families faced floods and blizzards.

In October, 1846, a wagon train with 87 settlers reached the Sierra Nevada mountains in northern California. They had met all of their difficulties bravely and hoped to be in California before winter. Many of their oxen had already been lost on the Great Salt Lake in Utah, but the families continued to struggle along on foot, pulling their wagons with them. A sudden blizzard caught them at the base of the mountain as they set up camp. It raged on for eight days, leaving Donner Pass blocked with snow drifts 40 feet high. Their camp was covered with freezing drifts, and their supplies ran out. Four months later, search parties found the families at their camp. Half of the men, women, and children had died. It was a sad ending for the brave group of settlers.

A hundred years later, a passenger train called *The City of San Francisco* was caught at the same place in another terrible blizzard. In January, 1952, 226 passengers and crewmen were crossing Donner Pass when 50-foot drifts and howling winds of snow stalled their train and blocked the pass. Lights and heat aboard the train went out as their fuel supply ran low. Food supplies soon ran out, and people began to use wooden seats and ladders to build small fires in the train cars for warmth. It took three days for rescue workers to reach the stranded passengers. No one died in that blizzard, but Donner Pass had once again caused a great deal of human misery.

1. Blizzards at Donner Pass are particularly dangerous because
    a. the snow drifts block the only path through the mountains.
    b. they only occur once in a hundred years.
    c. they last for just one day.
2. In October, 1846, the settlers probably
    a. didn't expect a snowstorm at Donner Pass that early in the season.
    b. were well-prepared for the blizzard in the mountains.
    c. knew the snowstorm was coming well ahead of time.
3. From the article, it is easy to see that
    a. snowstorms are rare in the Sierra Nevadas.
    b. trains are no longer allowed to cross the Sierra Nevadas.
    c. people can still be caught unexpectedly in dangerous mountain snowstorms.

Name _____

ICY WINTER DRIVING

You have read about some historical examples of extreme winter weather conditions, but every year people are affected by winter storms that are neither record-breaking nor unexpected. Over five thousand people have been killed by winter storms in the United States in the past fifty years. More than a thousand of these were automobile accidents. Many of them could have been avoided.

Even a thin layer of snow can make driving dangerous. As the snow melts, it often refreezes on the cold pavement to an icy glaze. Steering and brakes can be lost without notice. In the city, this is a hazard to the driver, passengers, and pedestrians. In isolated rural areas, even a minor accident can mean being stranded in the car as the storm increases.

In northern climates, food, heat and emergency supplies should be ready well ahead of winter's approach. Every car should also be ready for winter. Oil and antifreeze are necessities, but it is equally important to have brakes, heating systems, and tires carefully checked. Gas tanks should be kept full.

1. The best place to be during a winter storm is
   a. in your car.
   b. at home.
   c. at school.
2. Pedestrians can be endangered by winter driving because
   a. cars always stop for them at crosswalks.
   b. cars can't always stop on icy roads and may even slide up past curbs.
   c. they know the driver is always aware of hazardous conditions.
3. From this article, it is easy to see that
   a. winter driving causes many unnecessary deaths.
   b. it is fine to drive in the winter if you know what you are doing.
   c. driving on ice and snow is easy.

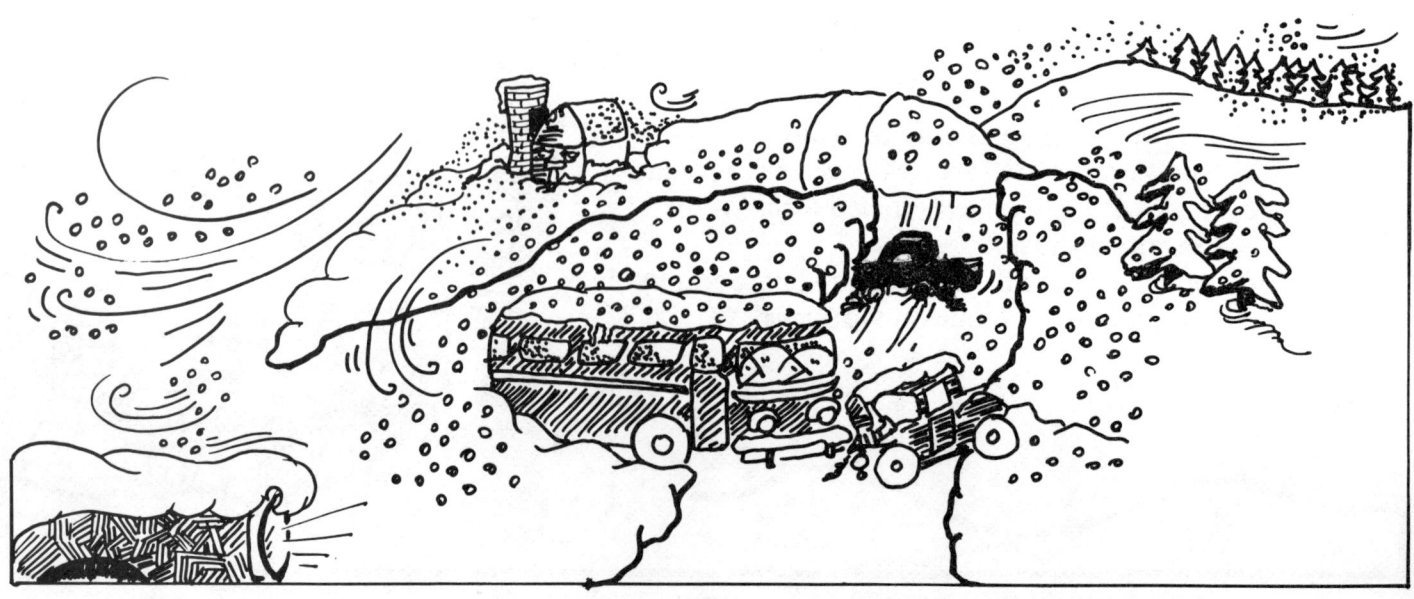

Name _____

WINTER STORM CAR KIT

It is obviously best not to travel at all when a winter storm is approaching, but in northern climates it is possible to be caught in an unexpected snowstorm. The National Oceanic and Atmospheric Administration (NOAA) suggests several items that should be carried in every car that might encounter icy weather. It is called a winter storm car kit. Items included are blankets or sleeping bags; extra clothing; matches; candle; paper towels; high calorie, nonperishable food; first aid kit; a canteen of water; shovel; a sack of sand; flashlight or signal light (with extra batteries); windshield scraper; booster cables; tow chains; fire extinguisher; catalytic heater; and axe.

There are additional safety rules to remember if a family is trapped in a stalled car during a snowstorm.

1. Stay in the car! It is never a good idea to walk for help in a blinding snowstorm. Even familiar paths can be hard to follow, especially at night.
2. Don't use the heater except for short periods when absolutely necessary. Be sure the care is well-ventilated!
3. Exercise by clapping hands and moving arms and legs briskly from time to time.
4. Be sure at least one person stays awake at all times.
5. Keep the dome light on at night so emergency crews can see the car.
6. Don't panic!

1. It is easy to lose your sense of direction in a snowstorm because
    a. you can see only a short distance, and everything is white.
    b. cold can affect your sight.
    c. familiar landmarks are always visible.
2. The sack of sand in the winter storm car kit would be helpful if you
    a. find a beach in the snowstorm.
    b. need to put sand under the car wheels for added traction.
    c. intend to make concrete.
3. From this article, it is easy to see that
    a. preparation is important at all times if you live in a winter climate.
    b. you only need a car kit if there is an immediate danger of storms.
    c. traveling in the winter is always safe and pleasant.

Name _____

WINTER KILLERS

People long ago learned the importance of dressing warmly against the bitter cold of winter. Early civilizations used animal skins and fur to protect their bodies from the wind and snow.

Most people today understand that, even with appropriate clothing, it is difficult for the body to withstand icy temperatures for long periods of time. It is especially dangerous to try heavy work for prolonged periods. The National Weather Service reports over a thousand deaths in the past fifty years from overexertion, exhaustion, and heart attacks during winter weather. Many of these fatalities could have been avoided.

Even healthy, physically strong people can be overwhelmed by **physical exertion** in extremely cold weather. It is more difficult to breath normally, the heart beats faster, and the body works harder to maintain a constant temperature. Shovelling snow, clearing driveways, and pushing heavy objects to remove them from deep snow are particularly dangerous.

Two other winter hazards are **hypothermia** and **frostbite**, especially when the windchill factor is high. When skin temperature falls to about 50° F, the loss of the sense of pain or touch is called hypoaesthesia. If part of the body continues to be exposed to cold, the blood vessels get smaller and blood circulation is impaired. Ice crystals begin to form within the tissue. Frostbite sets in. Permanent damage can result from frostbite, and sometimes fingers and toes must be amputated. One clue that provides warning ahead of frostbite is that the skin turns white, but this is hard to notice in boots and gloves, so people who are outdoors in cold and windy weather should be especially careful to protect themselves properly.

Hypothermia is almost always a killer. A normally healthy person's temperature is 98.6°. If the body termperature falls below 90°, a person goes into a coma and can no longer move towards shelter or protection. Just before that, all sense of pain, direction, or recognition of danger ceases; the person only wants to sleep. It's important to keep moving and to maintain circulation if you are caught in the cold for extended periods.

Icy water is another winter hazard. A person dies within seven minutes in water 35° F, but even in slightly warmer water, loss of body heat is 23 times faster in water than in air. Hypothermia can cause death in water 58° F for even a short period of time.

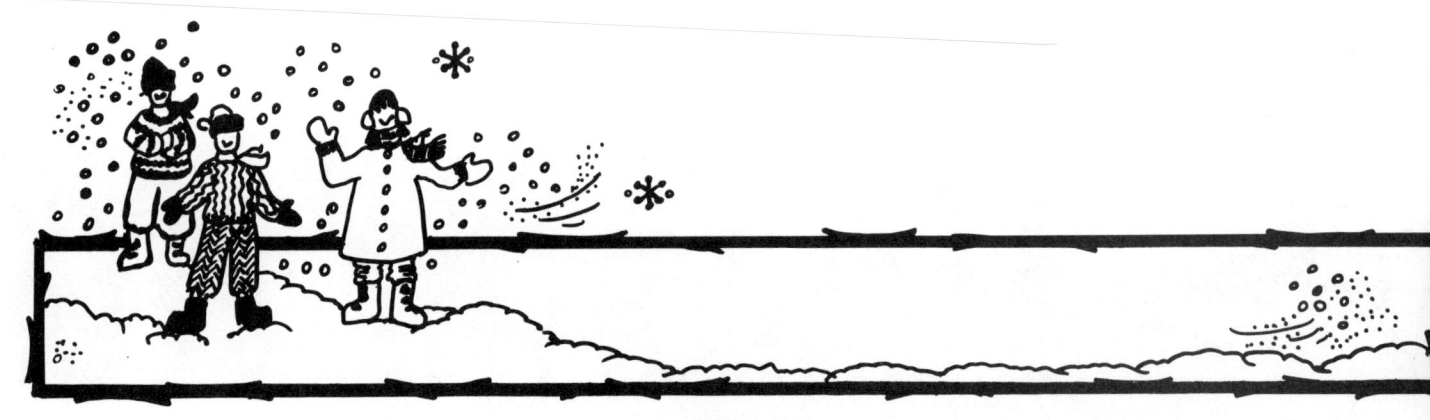

Name _____

WINDCHILL FACTOR

Gentle midmorning breezes that stir off lakes and seas during warm summer months help cool families along the shores. By evaporating water from people as they sunbathe, work in gardens, or stroll along the beaches, they bring pleasant relief when the temperature and humidity are high.

As temperatures drop and the winds increase, the effects of cooling make people much less comfortable. A person walking to the store, dressed for winter, in 20° weather will feel the same chilling effect as if the air were -18° F when the wind speed is 30 miles per hour. This is called the **windchill factor**. It is a much more accurate way for people to choose the amount of protection they'll need for winter days. Most weather reports include the windchill factor in their bulletins and forecasts.

The National Weather Service publishes the following chart (NOAA/PA 79015) to help determine windchill. Find the outside temperature on the top line, then read down the column to the measured wind speed. Temperatures are recorded in Fahrenheit.

Wind Speed (mph)	35	30	25	20	15	10	5	0	-5	-10	-15	-20	-25	-30
5	32	27	22	16	11	6	0	-5	-10	-15	-21	-26	-31	-36
10	22	16	10	3	-3	-9	-15	-22	-27	-34	-40	-46	-52	-58
15	16	9	2	-5	-11	-18	-25	-31	-38	-45	-51	-58	-65	-72
20	12	4	-3	-10	-17	-24	-31	-39	-46	-53	-60	-67	-74	-81
25	8	1	-7	-15	-22	-29	-36	-44	-51	-59	-66	-74	-81	-88
30	6	-2	-10	-18	-25	-33	-41	-49	-56	-64	-71	-79	-86	-93
35	4	-4	-12	-20	-27	-35	-43	-52	-58	-67	-74	-82	-89	-97

See if you can dress these children warmly according to the windchill factor as they wait for the school bus. Use the chart to find the windchill temperatures.

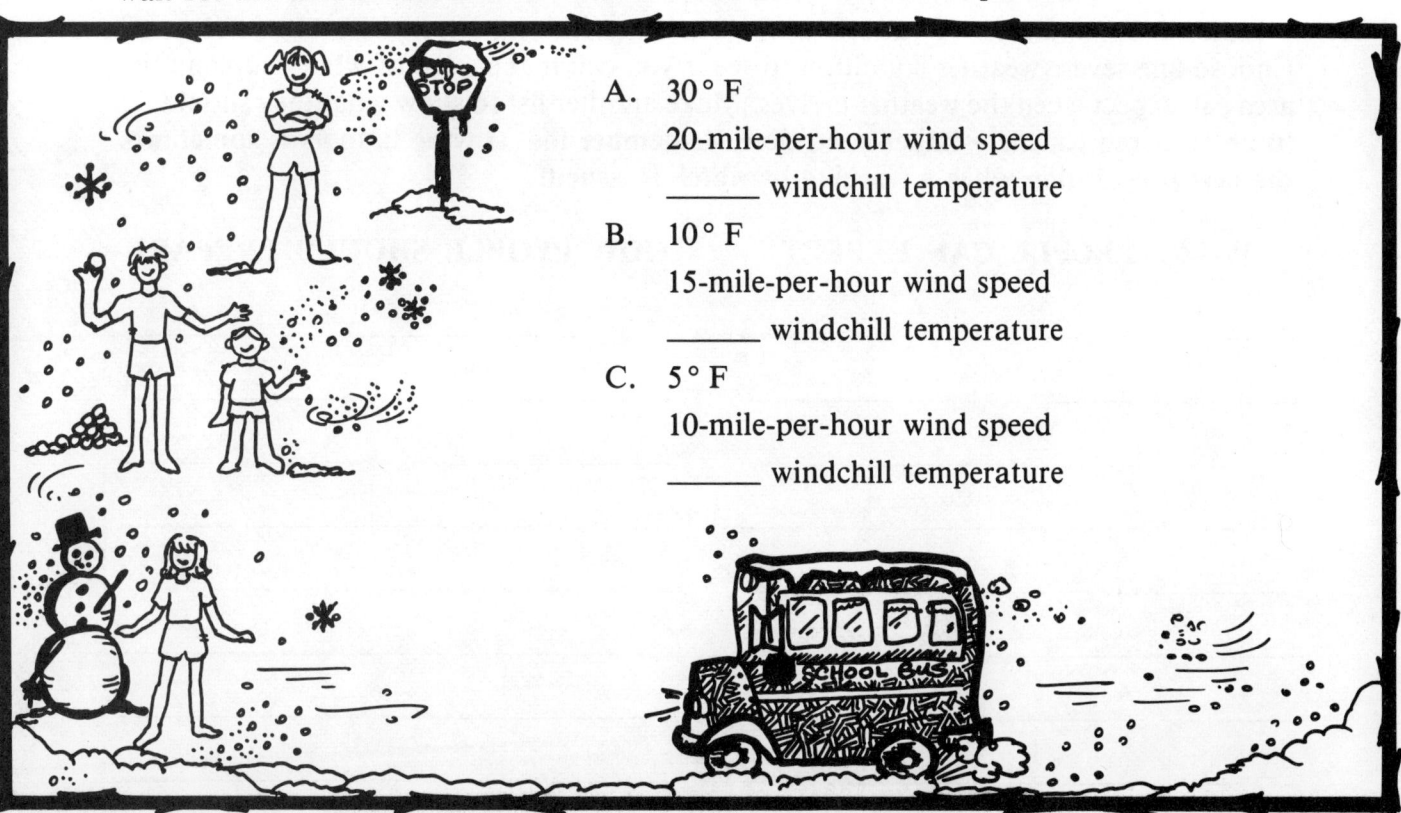

A. 30° F
   20-mile-per-hour wind speed
   _____ windchill temperature

B. 10° F
   15-mile-per-hour wind speed
   _____ windchill temperature

C. 5° F
   10-mile-per-hour wind speed
   _____ windchill temperature

Name _____

WEATHER WATCH AND WARNINGS

When hazardous weather is approaching an area, the National Weather Service issues special warnings and watches so people can prepare for winter storms. It is a good idea to keep a list of what each weather warning means if your house is located in an area that is likely to be affected by severe winter weather.

Winter Storm Watch means severe winter weather conditions like freezing rain, sleet or heavy snow may affect your area soon.
Winter Storm Warning means severe weather conditions are definitely in your area right now!
Heavy Snow Warning means a snowfall of at least four inches in twelve hours is expected. If you live in an area that doesn't usually get much snow, this warning may mean a little less than four inches.
Blizzard Warning means that large amounts of snowfall and blowing snow with winds of at least 35 miles per hour are expected for several hours.
High Wind Warning means that winds of at least 40 miles per hour are expected to last for at least one hour.
Freezing Rain and **Freezing Drizzle** warn people that a coating of ice is expected on the ground and other exposed surfaces. Electric and communication services may be disrupted when ice coats trees and wires.

How many of these hazardous warnings and watches have you heard in your area? Choose one severe weather condition to see if you can make a list of what people in the area can expect when the weather arrives. Make another list to show what they should do to be prepared for the weather condition. **Remember that staying indoors is sometimes the best preparation when a warning or watch is issued!**

WHAT PEOPLE CAN EXPECT	HOW PEOPLE SHOULD PREPARE
_____	_____
_____	_____
_____	_____
_____	_____
_____	_____
_____	_____
_____	_____

Name _____

WINTER STORM SAFETY RULES

The National Oceanic and Atmospheric Administration (NOAA) suggests that the best way to protect life and property during a winter storm is to be prepared! If you live in an area that usually has heavy snows and bitter cold spells, be prepared for winter well ahead of time.
1. Check battery-powered radio, television, flashlight, heating equipment, and cooking equipment carefully. Make sure that everything is in good working order. Always have extra batteries on hand. Be sure batteries are fresh in equipment that has not been used for awhile.
2. Never let heating fuel in your home run low. If a major storm strikes your area, it may be a long time before fuel service returns to normal. Have an alternate heating source handy for emergencies.
3. Be sure your pantry is well-stocked with food supplies that need no cooking or refrigeration.

You have read about the dangers of getting caught in your car during blizzards or icy weather. You know that overexertion and hypothermia are deadly winter dangers. All of these winter killers can be avoided if you and your family are prepared for winter weather and have taken the time to plan ahead for severe weather conditions.

1. Battery-powered equipment is especially important during a winter storm because
   a. electric power is likely to be interrupted by icy lines and fallen trees.
   b. you get better reception on battery-operated radios during a snowstorm.
   c. it's easier to carry it with you if you go out in the storm.
2. The best way to protect yourself during a winter storm is probably
   a. the preparation you make ahead of time.
   b. to wear mittens when you go out to chop wood.
   c. running to the store after you've heard a storm alert.
3. From this article, it is easy to see that
   a. there is usually some warning before a major winter storm.
   b. there is usually no warning before a major winter storm.
   c. the Weather Service cannot accurately watch for winter storms.

Name _____

WINTER WEATHER WORD SEARCH

```
S L E E T R E T N I W
N S E I R R U L F S P
O V C Z L O U D U L W
W I N D O Z Z O L G A
S T O R M M D T R O T
E R N I A R S U P V C
Z M C Z A I L L I A H
E E S Z M V N R O M T
E N A L B L O W I N G
R R K B L I Z Z A R D
F L A K E S P O L A R
```

See if you can find some of these winter weather words in the word search on the left. Words may run vertically, horizontally, or diagonally, backwards or forwards.

arctic	polar	sleet
snow	wind	drizzle
flurries	freeze	rain
storm	ice	watch
drift	cloud	hazardous
mist	blizzard	blowing
cold	winter	fog
hail	flakes	

38

Name _____

MEASURING HEAT AND COLD

Weather forecasting is both an **art** and a **science**. You have seen how hundreds of mathematical computations are made by computers to weigh and compare all the information available to determine what kind of weather is on the way. That is the science part of weather forecasting.

The art of weather forecasting has developed through the contributions of thousands of dedicated scientists, philosophers, inventors, and ordinary people interested in knowing more about the weather. Careful weather records have only been made over the past two hundred years. Early records came from farmers, seamen, and families in small villages throughout the United States and Europe. Many individual observations are still the basis of weather reporting and predicting. Each piece of information must be carefully weighed.

The invention of the thermometer was one of the first steps towards modern weather studies. Gabriel **Fahrenheit** (1686-1736) put mercury in a glass tube to develop a thermometer much like those people use today. His scale of degrees goes from 32° (the melting point of ice) to 212° (the boiling point of water). The °F after a temperature tells that it is in Fahrenheit.

Anders **Celsius** (1701-1744) tried to make the Fahrenheit scale metric. He suggested that zero° should be the boiling point of water and 100° should be the melting point of ice. The bigger the number, according to Celsius' first scale, the colder the temperature. This was just the opposite direction from scales already in use. Scientists liked the idea of using a metric scale, however, so they turned Celsius upside down and adopted it immediately.

Today, both systems for recording temperatures are used around the world. Celcius degrees are written °C. The melting point of ice is 0°C, and 100°C is the boiling point of water. Sometimes this scale is called **centigrade**.

1. Scientists adopted the Celsius temperature scale because
   a. it was more accurate.
   b. it made calculations easier because it was based on the metric 1 to 100.
   c. Celsius talked them into it.
2. The art of weather forecasting is based on the importance of
   a. mathematical computations.
   b. human experience and judgment.
   c. computers.
3. From this article it is easy to see that
   a. weather reporting and forecasting started to become more scientific with the development of measuring instruments.
   b. people use only one temperature scale.
   c. centigrade is the same as Fahrenheit.

ANSWER KEY

p. 4	1. b, 2. b, 3. b	p. 24	1. b, 2. a, 3. b
p. 6	1. a, 2. c, 3. c	p. 25	1. a, 2. a, b, c, 3. b
p. 7	1. b, 2. b, 3. c	p. 26	1. a, 2. a, 3. c
p. 8	1. a, 2. b, 3. a	p. 27	1. b, 2. c, 3. b
p. 12	cloud, thunder, turbulence, lightning, atmosphere, stable, mile, cumulonimbus (e, a, and t are letters used very frequently)	p. 28	1. a, 2. a, 3. c
		p. 30	1. c, 2. a, 3. c
		p. 31	1. a, 2. a, 3. c
p. 13	1. a, 2. b, 3. a	p. 32	1. b, 2. b, 3. a
p. 14	1. c, 2. b, 3. a	p. 33	1. a, 2. b, 3. a
p. 15	1. b, 2. a, 3. a	p. 35	a. 4° b. -18° c. -15°
p. 18	1. a, 2. b, 3. b		
p. 20	1. a, 2. b, 3. c	p. 36	Answers will vary.
p. 21	A. stellar B. hexagonal capped column C. graupel D. hexagonal column E. stellar F. graupel G. ice needles H. hexagonal plates I. asymmetrical crystals J. stellar	p. 37	1. a, 2. a, 3. a
		p. 39	1. b, 2. b, 3. a

Weather reporting and forecasting is not yet perfected. It is a vital and changing area with mysteries yet unsolved. As students discover more about winter storms and blizzards, they are encouraged to participate in group discussions and to independently consider their own roles in understanding weather, adapting to its changes, and considering their choices, consequences, and alternatives that affect weather. These are open-ended opportunities encompassing creative problem solving and future decision making. Their answers may well be some of our most innovative answers for the future.

INDEX

adaption (25)
atmosphere (8)
Arctic fox (25)
autumnal equinox (7)
avalanche (17)
Bentley, William A. (20)
bergy bits (17)
blizzards (29-31)
climate (6)
coldest place in world (16)
cumulonimbus (11)
de Paola, Tomie (22)
Donner Pass (31)
downdrafts (11)
drifts (29)
driving in winter (32)
droughts (6)
dry snow (17)
edelweiss (18)
elliptical (7)
equinox (7)
flurries (29)
forecasting weather (2, 28, 36)
forest fires (13)
freezing rain (16, 36)
Frost, Robert (22)
frostbite (34)
glaciers (17)
Grand Canyon Suite (13)
graupel (17)
greenhouse effect (8)
growlers (17)
gust (9)
hail (11, 17)
hailstones (11, 17)
hibernation (24)
hypothermia (34)
ice cream (16)
ice shelf (17)

leader strokes (13)
lightning (11, 13)
local winds (9)
low pressure system (26)
lull (9)
migration (24)
monitoring winter weather (28)
motif (23)
overexertion (34)
permafrost (17)
permanent ice sheet (16)
photomicrographs (20)
polar air (26)
Rankin, William H. (15)
root words (19)
safety precautions
    lightning (14)
    winter driving (33)
    winter storm (37)
snow, snowflakes (16, 17, 20)
solstice (7)
squalls (29)
storm patterns in U.S. (26)
surface winds (9)
Theophrastus (2)
thunder (11)
thunderstorms (11)
topography (6)
trade winds (9)
tropical air (26)
turbulence (9, 26)
updrafts (11)
vernal equinox (7)
weather fronts (9)
westerlies (9)
wet snow (17)
windchill (35)
winter dangers (32-34)
winter storm warnings (36)

BIBLIOGRAPHY

Battan, Louis J. *Weather in Your Life*. New York: W. H. Freeman and Company, 1983.
Bova, Ben. *Man Changes the Weather*. Addison Wesley, 1973.
DeBruin, Jerry. *Creative, Hands-on Science Experiences*. Carthage, Ill.: Good Apple, Inc., 1980.
Davis, Hubert. *A January Fog Will Freeze a Hog*. New York: Crown Publishers, 1977.
Holford, Ingrid. *Weather Facts and Feats*. Sterling Publishing Co., 1977.
Jobb, Jamie. *The Night Sky Book*. Boston: Little, Brown, and Company, 1977.
Thompson, Phillip D., and Robert O'Brien. *Weather*. Time-Life Books, 1965.
Collins Young Scientist's Book of Cold. Morristown, N.J.: Silver Burdett, 1976.